This book is dedicated to all the brave kids battling cancer and every other debilitating, and/or life-threatening illness. Special love to all the doctors, nurses, and families in 5 Tower & IP 7 at NYP-Morgan Stanley Children's Hospital, The Ronald McDonald House, and in our world beyond…

You are beautiful.
You are loved.
We are you.

Sending love, sending light, sending strength…

Love,

aryn

As far back as she could think,

Aryn's mommy would brush her thick, soft,

curly brown hair.

And then top it off with a *bow!*

she had blue bows,
pink bows,
even sparkly bows,

———————— Aryn *loved* bows ————————

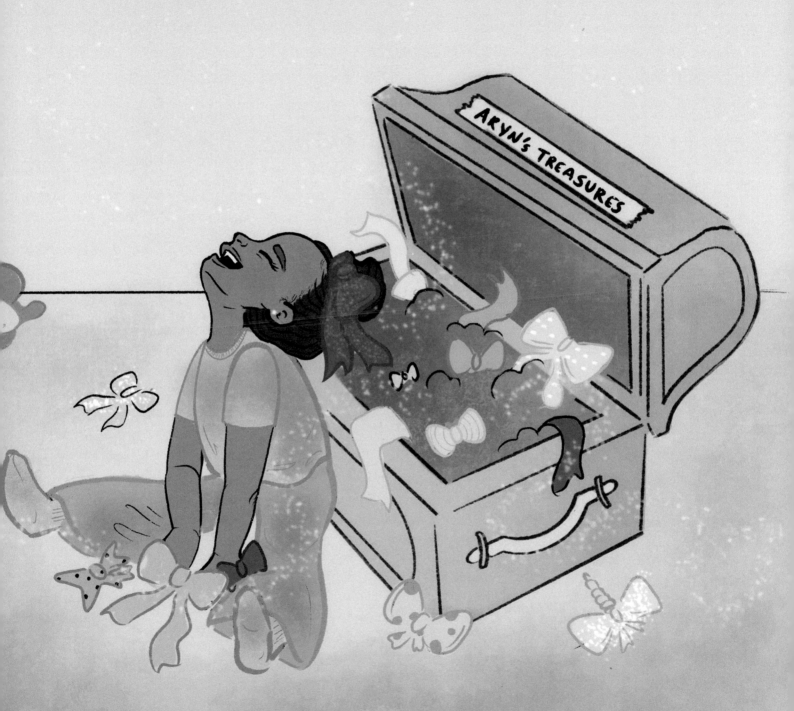

As Aryn grew older
her hair finally grew long enough to add

beads and braids.

these were not just plain

beads and braids

they were

Magical.

And any little girl who wore them received
special powers.

the power of movement

the power of wisdom

the power of

imagination

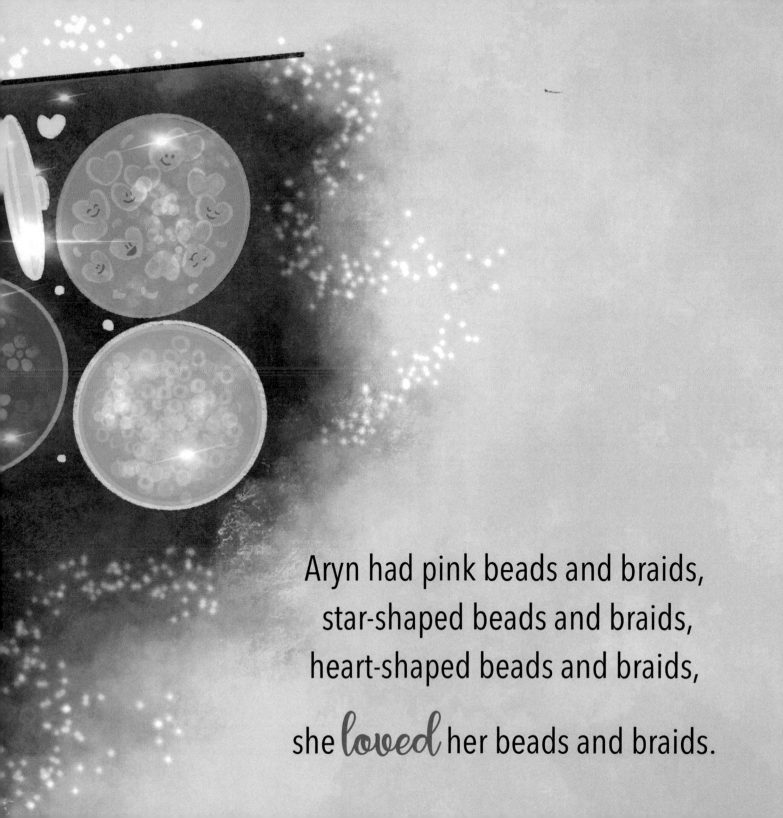

Aryn had pink beads and braids,
star-shaped beads and braids,
heart-shaped beads and braids,

she *loved* her beads and braids.

One day Aryn got very sick and
she had to go to the hospital for
a long time.

"Baby, mommy is here.
I believe that you are going to be just fine.
You will lose your hair, you will have some
rough moments, I love you and I am

not going anywhere."

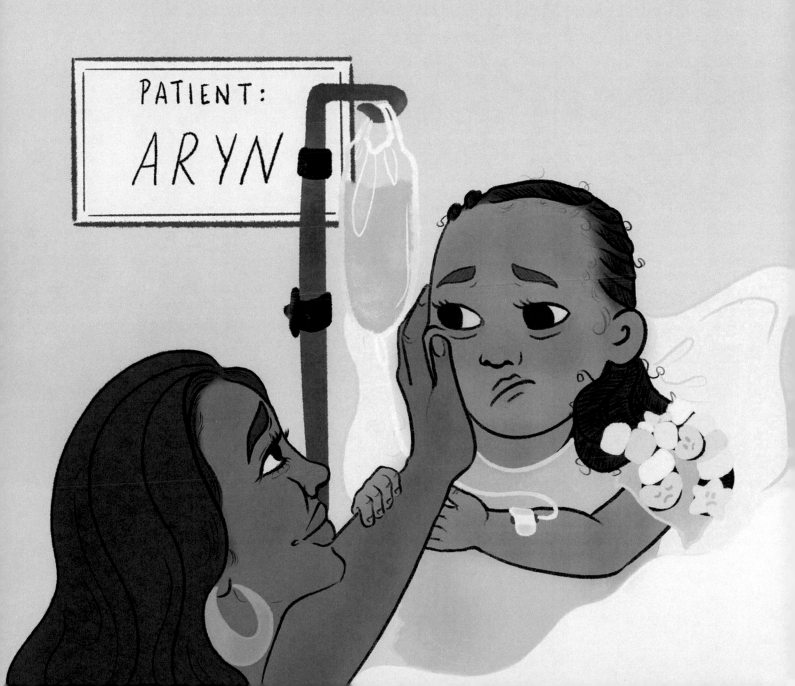

Aryn had some rough moments,
Aryn's hair fell out, and Aryn felt alone.

My child will make it, I believe in her healing.
I will be there.
Aryn, you are not alone.

Aryn put on a pink bow,
a *purple bow*.
a *leopard bow*.
even a *squiggly bow*.

But none of them fit quite like her beads and braids.

Aryn started to get better,
she grew

bigger and stronger

And stronger and bigger,

and so did her hair

Aryn's hair just kept growing and growing and

growing...

And one day her mommy said:
"Baby, I think it's time for some
beads and braids!"

Aryn looked at her mommy and said:

"Yes, I missed my beads and braids…

and I'm glad to have them again but I've learned

that the super power of the beads and braids was

inside my heart all along

Aryn, her mommy, her daddy, her baby brother,
AND her beads and braids,
lived happily. healthily. after.

The End.

Made in the USA
Middletown, DE
04 September 2020